Greater Than a To Durban KwaZulu-Natal South Africa

50 Travel Tips from a Local

Nazeera Rawat

Copyright © 2017 CZYK Publishing

All Rights Reserved. No part of this publication may be reproduced, including scanning and photocopying, or distributed in any form or by any means, electronic or mechanical, or stored in a database or retrieval system without prior written permission from the publisher.

Disclaimer: The publisher has put forth an effort in preparing and arranging this book. The information provided herein by the author is provided "as is". Use this information at your own risk. The publisher is not a licensed doctor. Consult your doctor before engaging in any medical activities. The publisher and author disclaim any liabilities for any loss of profit or commercial or personal damages resulting from the information contained in this book.

Order Information: To order this title please email lbrenenc@gmail.com or visit GreaterThanATourist.com. A bulk discount can be provided.

CZYK
PUBLISHING

Lock Haven, PA

All rights reserved.
ISBN: 9781521869789

>TOURIST
50 TRAVEL TIPS FROM A LOCAL

Nazeera Rawat

BOOK DESCRIPTION

Are you excited about planning your next trip?

Do you want to try something new while traveling?

Would you like some guidance from a local?

If you answered yes to any of these questions, then this book is just for you.

Greater Than a Tourist – Durban, South Africa by Nazeera Rawat offers the inside scope on Durban, South Africa. Most travel books tell you how to travel like a tourist. Although there's nothing wrong with that, as a part of the Greater than a Tourist series, this book will give you travel tips from someone who lives at your next travel destination.

In these pages you'll discover local advice that will help you throughout your stay. Greater than a Tourist is a series of travel books written by locals. Travel like a local. Slow down, stay in one place, and get to know the people and the culture of a place. By the time you finish this book, you will be excited and prepared to travel to your next destination.

Nazeera Rawat

TABLE OF CONTENTS

BOOK DESCRIPTION

TABLE OF CONTENTS

DEDICATION

FROM THE PUBLISHER

WELCOME TO > TOURIST

INTRODUCTION

1. Best Time To Visit
2. Where Should I Stay?
3. Getting Around
4. Eating Your Way Through Town, Even On A Budget!
5. Swing The Big Rush Big Swing – Tallest In The World!
6. View The Beach From Above
7. Experience A 360° View (While Revolving!) Of Durban
8. Ride The Waves
9. Spend The Weekend Exploring Ushaka Marine World
10. Dine Like The Godfather, An Offer You Can't Refuse!
11. Browse A Morning Market
12. Buy Handmade Proudly South African Merchandise
13. Release Your Inner Child At Funworld
14. Stroll Wilson's Wharf
15. Wake Up Early To Watch The Sunrise!

16. Hike A Nature Trail
17. Visit Howick Falls And Get A Waffle On A Stick
18. Experience A Bit Of History At The Mandela Capture Site
19. Take A Vintage Train Through The Valley Of 1000 Hills
20. Drink Coffee As Fresh As It Gets!
21. Saddle Up And Explore The Midland Meander
22. Bike The Golden Mile
23. Shop Till You Drop At Gateway: Theatre Of Shopping
24. Get In The Sporting Spirit
25. Spot The Big 5 On Safari Featuring An African Sunset!
27. Appreciate Some Of The Best And Funniest Sand Art Around
28. Take A Rickshaw Ride, You Won't Regret It
29. Cruise The Indian Ocean
30. Rent Out A House At Zimbali
31. Hit A Hole In One!
32. Spend A Night At The Races
33. Catch A Fish, There Are Plenty!
34. Wander The Art District
35. Attend An Expo
36. Book A Weekend At The Drakensburg Mountains
37. Explore Durban's Historical Sites, Architecture and Museums

38. Feel Like A Giant As You Walk Mini Town!

39. Tweet Surrounded By 100's Of Species Of Birds

40. Picnic At Mitchell Park

41. Rock Out To Local Music Every Sunday at Botanical Gardens

42. Glam Up For The Durban July Event!

43. Hop On The Durban City Open Top Bus Tour

44. Soak Up Panoramic Views From The Cube Lookout

45. Join An AstroTurf Soccer Match

46. Treat Yourself To A Spa Day At Camp Orchids

47. Zip-Line Across Oribi Gorge

48. Explore Castle On Main

49. Light Up Your Life At The Umhlanga Lighthouse

50. Water Sport To Your Hearts Content

Top Reasons to Book This Trip

WHERE WILL YOU TRAVEL TO NEXT?

Our Story

Notes

DEDICATION

This book is dedicated to my friends and family. For always giving me love and attention, no matter how much I needed! It is also dedicated to my cat, Salem, for coming home ALMOST every night during the past 12 years.

Nazeera Rawat

ABOUT THE AUTHOR

Nazeera Rawat is an avid photographer, cat lover and dreamer who lives Durban, South Africa. She has a Postgraduate degree in Psychology and loves to read, be creative and expand her horizons.

Nazeera loves to travel and is slowly ticking places off her very long list of must see places around the world. She loves to experience places from a non-conventional angle.

Nazeera likes to connect with people who are from the places she visits beforehand by utilizing the internet and joining online communities. It's the best way to experience the real love people have for their homes and enjoy all things local!

Nazeera is a born and bred Durbanite and knows how to have the best Durban experience! As they say in South Africa, Local is Lekker!

Nazeera Rawat

HOW TO USE THIS BOOK

This book was written by someone who has lived in an area for over three months. The author has made the best suggestions based on their own experiences in the area. Please check that these places are still available before traveling to the area. The goal of this book is to help travelers either dream or experience different locations by providing opinions from a local.

Nazeera Rawat

FROM THE PUBLISHER

Traveling can be one of the most important moments in a person's life. The memories that you have of anticipating going somewhere new or getting to travel are some of the best. As a publisher of the Greater Than a Tourist book series, as well as the popular 50 Things to Know book series, we strive to help you learn about new places, spark your imagination, and inspire you.

Thought this book you will find something for every traveler. Wherever you are and whatever you do I wish you safe fun, and inspiring travel.

Lisa Rusczyk Ed. D.
CZYK Publishing

Nazeera Rawat

>TOURIST

WELCOME TO > TOURIST

Nazeera Rawat

INTRODUCTION

My favourite part of travelling or having people visit me in my home town is getting the experience you wouldn't usually get otherwise. When you live in a place for a very long time you discover things you wouldn't by just spending a few weeks there.

Often a local doesn't even realise they are privy to so many amazing spots or restaurants because it can seem like just part of your everyday life! Little do they know a visitor would relish to be immersed in your local culture and local life, sometimes it's the little things that make the biggest impact on your memory of your holiday.

I love to make friends online so I end up with the opportunity to experience many different things in the countries I've visited over the years. The flipside of that is that when they visit me in South Africa I get to host them and show them why I LOVE Durban! The best part is that sometimes in accommodating a friend I learn new things about my city too!

Durban is a little, or not so little, beach town on the east coast of South Africa. We are very culturally diverse with the Indian culture and tradition having a strong impact on all the locals no matter their colour or religion! One thing I have learnt over the years is that we eat all our food really spicy! It surprised me to learn that a little bowl of crushed chili is NOT served at every restaurant around the world no matter your meal.

In Durban, and in South Africa generally, we are very into sport. It is common to see people out and about on normal days wearing supporters merchandise. The whole city tries to turn up for games and the atmosphere is really infectious!

Durban is known for being the friendliest city in South Africa so you will never have to worry about not having a good time here even if you choose to travel alone. Because of our laid back beach vibe it's the perfect place to take a relaxed holiday while still getting a sense of adventure! The term Local is Lekker, lekker meaning nice or good in Afrikaans, was coined as something to inspire pride in our nation, a sense of unity to truly show off our rainbow nation and all it has to offer.

>TOURIST

Besides our easy going beachy vibes, Durban and surrounds also has strong historical value. One place being the site of one of the most significant points in our history, the Capture of Nelson Mandel which led to his 27 years of imprisonment!

Whether you're looking for the beach, history or both, fun and sun will greet you on your arrival!

Nazeera Rawat

1. Best Time To Visit

The best part about Durban is that it is ALWAYS a good time to visit. We have great weather all year around with hot summers and mild winters. An amazing selling point being the Indian Ocean! Guaranteeing warm water and fun in the sun no matter the time of year or season. 365 beach days a year anyone?

2. Where Should I Stay?

Finding somewhere to stay in Durban is very easy. We have a coast lined with hotels end to end, both on the frontline (beach facing) and second row (no beach view). Besides the beach hotels there are many other hotels in the city and outlying areas. I personally prefer staying right on the beach. It is convenient and allows you to enjoy the sea air and view on those lazy days without leaving your room! There are also private apartments and houses by the beach that you can book with a little internet research.

3. Getting Around

Getting around can become difficult if you don't know which types of transport to use. Ubers are popular but are not the only way to travel around the city. We do not have a good train service so your best bet would be vehicles. It's important to distinguish between a taxi and a cab, a cab is the type of transport you call when you need a ride somewhere, commonly called a taxi in other parts of the world. In South Africa a taxi is a very low cost form of transport most commonly used by the locals. You will easily recognize these as they tend to be 12 seater shuttle like vehicles. Another good way to get around the beach area and main city are buses called People Movers. These buses have regular stops and run long hours. Your most luxurious option would be to hire a car and drive around. This is a great option as parking is easy to find on the beach and is free! Just remember, here in South Africa we drive on the left!

4. Eating Your Way Through Town, Even On A Budget!

Durbanites love to eat! There are countless places to eat no matter your budget or preferences. Durban has 2 signature dishes that are a must eat if visiting the city, Durban Curry and Bunny Chow! Don't be alarmed, no bunnies are harmed in the making of Bunny Chow, in fact it is a vegan dish. Other places to try include the Cargo Hold where you dine amoung Sharks at the Marine World Shark Tank, Surf Riders Beach Café which serves vegan dishes and Haute Tea at the Oyster Box.

If you're looking for atmospheric nighttime dining then Florida Road is the perfect street to get your fix! If halal fast food or Indian Cuisine is what you crave then visit Sparks Road and you will be spoiled for choice. The most economical way of making sure you get all your meals AND save money is to visit a supermarket every few days and stock up on ingredients or foods that are easy to make and won't spoil.

5. Swing The Big Rush Big Swing – Tallest In The World!

Visit Durban's world famous Moses Mabhida Stadium to get a unique Durban experience. This is home to the tallest swing in the world. Climb up the side of the stadiums handle to a platform high above the field, strap in and then…jump off! It's a rush!

6. View The Beach From Above

While you're at the stadium make sure you ride the Sky Car to the viewing deck located at the apex of the 'basket handle'. This deck allows you to get amazing views of the coast from high above it all! Ride up and stay as long as you like, the car goes up and down every half hour.

7. Experience A 360° View (While Revolving!) Of Durban

Yes! You read right! Roma Revolving Restaurant is located on the Esplanade near the Durban Yacht Club. You can enjoy a lovely meal whilst getting an amazing view of Durban. As you revolve you will see the harbor, beach and inland toward the city and suburbs. Bookings are required and prices are average to high but it is well worth it! Don't worry if you are prone to motion sickness, I am too but you barely feel any movement.

As long as you don't pay too much attention to it, like staring at the floor where you can see the boundary between the revolving deck and stationary deck, you'll be completely fine. Don't forget your camera!

8. Ride The Waves

A big attraction in Durban are the waves. Our beaches are a favourite spot for surfers and people who like to enjoy water sports. A day doesn't go by where you do not see surfers, jet skis, kayaks, yachts or windsurfers relishing the sun and warm Indian Ocean. There is a surfing club where you can get a few lessons before hitting the waves yourself but if that's not your style (it isn't mine either) I also enjoy sitting on the beach and watching the surfers or walking one of our many piers to get a closer look at the action!

9. Spend The Weekend Exploring Ushaka Marine World

Located at the southern end of Durban's coast line is Ushaka Marine World. There are quite a few things you can do here and it would probably take you a whole weekend if you wanted to do everything. The main attractions here are the Aquarium, Wet 'n Wild Water park and a small mall full of restaurants, surfing shops and African style souvenirs. You can also swim with the sharks or watch feedings, see a dolphin show or venture into the Dangerous Creatures Exhibit. There is enclosed pay parking on site if you prefer to take your own transport. Alternatively, Ushaka is a stop on the People Mover Bus Route.

10. Dine Like The Godfather, An Offer You Can't Refuse!

A unique experience is stopping for a bite at The Vapour Café. This café is themed after The Godfather movies and boasts a menu headed 'The Hit List' with meals named after characters from the movies. This café is perfect no matter the time of day, it always has a good vibe!

>TOURIST

Nazeera Rawat

>TOURIST

"Where ever you go, go with all your heart."

– Confucius

Nazeera Rawat

11. Browse A Morning Market

A favourite activity of mine as well as countless other Durbanites! Morning Markets are a huge thing here and so there are many to choose from. If you'd like a bite to eat after your early morning Sunday run (or just want food pronto) then a good place to stop at would be The Morning Trade, an organic and specialty food market. It has everything, from coconut water served in actual coconuts to gourmet cupcakes!

The only downside is that you have to be an early bird or you'll miss the worm (which I have done many times!). If you're looking for something more than just food then make sure to visit the iHeart Market located on the grounds of Moses Mabhida Stadium every first Saturday of the month. Here you will find food (of course) as well as handmade wares, upcoming designer clothes and vintage or antique items. It's the perfect place to find something one of a kind!

12. Buy Handmade Proudly South African Merchandise

Another place to buy something handmade is along the beach. Here there are countless local vendors who set up stalls and sell their wares. It's a great place to get an authentic handmade African souvenir. From experience I can tell you it's also a lifesaver in a beach related emergency such as breaking your flip flops or messing your shirt with ice cream!

13. Release Your Inner Child At Funworld

Right on the beach is a small attraction that has fun rides, bumper cars and arcade games available for all ages. The ride people like most in this small theme park is the sky carriage, which takes you on a short ride high above the park! This is great for couples and kids love it to. A word of warning though: make sure to wear shoes that are firmly attached to your feet or they will fall off somewhere above the park and you will struggle to find them again!

14. Stroll Wilson's Wharf

If you're looking for a low key outing or just want to start your day off nice and slow or relaxing then Wilson's Wharf is a good place to go. Built on the water and housing some restaurants and shops you can have a chilled out breakfast or lunch while breathing in the fresh sea air and enjoying the view. There are also a few activities you can book from ticket offices located here, like sea life tours, short cruises on the harbor or a morning on a yacht out at sea.

15. Wake Up Early To Watch The Sunrise!

The best thing about this tip is that it's free and AMAZING. Have you ever seen a sunrise? Now have you ever seen the sun rise over the Indian Ocean slowly lighting up the beach, the awakening of the birds, the waves dotted with early morning surfers? This is something I love and never get tired of doing. As someone who has spent their whole life in Durban, I'm still excited to see a sunrise like this every time. No matter how many times I've seen it, I always want to see it again!

16. Hike A Nature Trail

This is also something you can do for free depending on your level of confidence hiking. There are trails that anyone can just hike or you can go with a guide on a guided hike. Hikes are readily available almost everywhere in Durban and the surrounding areas. It's a city lush with vegetation, rivers and protected areas which are perfect for hiking!

17. Visit Howick Falls And Get A Waffle On A Stick

Howick Falls is our very own little waterfall a couple of hours drive out of Durban. Here you can hike, walk under the falls or swim. If you leave early and don't mind returning after dark then this activity is easily done in one day. Don't forget to stop at a vendor that sells delicious waffles on a stick with a variety of toppings and dips, a sweet treat after your hike.

18. Experience A Bit Of History At The Mandela Capture Site

Also a couple of hours drive out of Durban, this little slice of earth marks a very important day and place in South African history. The exact location of the road block that led to Nelson Mandela's arrest and subsequent 27 years of imprisonment. It is marked by an artistic installation, a monument celebrating our great leader, and is accompanied by a small museum.

Even if you are not a history buff the artist designed his installation in a very creative way. If you stand in one exact spot the metal spires converge to form the iconic picture of Mr Mandela's face.

19. Take A Vintage Train Through The Valley Of 1000 Hills

One of the last operating steam engine trains takes you on a scenic ride through the Midlands Meander and Valley of 1000 Hills. With spectacular views and a 1 hour stop to picnic this is an amazing family outing for children of all ages and even adults! Ever wanted to ride the Hogwarts Express? Here's your chance! There are also souvenir shops, some food stalls and bathroom facilities at the stop.

20. Drink Coffee As Fresh As It Gets!

A short drive out of the city and you hit an area called Assagay. This is an area known for its farms, in particular, coffee bean farms! You will have to book in advance for a tour of any one of the many coffee bean farms available. On the tour they will take you through the whole process of coffee making, from growing the plants to bottling the coffee you find on your table! The tour usually ends with a sampling of fresh coffee in various strengths. You can also buy bags of coffee and other homemade products such as coffee soaps and coffee flavoured fudge.

>TOURIST

"We shall not cease from exploration, and the end of all our loring will be to arrive where we started and know the place for the first time."

– T.S Elliot

Nazeera Rawat

21. Saddle Up And Explore The Midland Meander

Go horseback riding through the Midlands Meander. This is a very scenic and beautiful area that has a river and some wildlife that you could spot on your ride. Be one with nature and take in the fresh air and sun while not having to do much work yourself! If you prefer not to take a horse out you can still take short rides within estates. Make it a family affair too!

22. Bike The Golden Mile

It is very common to see people biking up and down our paved coast line from North to South or vice versa, we call this the Golden Mile. It is lined with hotels and restaurants and paved all the way down both sides.

The promenade is always full of people skateboarding, rollerblading or just plain walking and running. What people don't realise is that you can hire bikes hourly at either side if you don't own your own bike! You can even go a little further and join up at Moses Mabhida Stadium.

23. Shop Till You Drop At Gateway: Theatre Of Shopping

Gateway is the biggest mall we have to offer in Durban. It's about 20 minutes from the beachfront. Besides the usual shops and restaurants, this mall has some unique features. One is that there is a theatre inside the mall that regularly puts on plays, shows and concerts.

Another is an indoor wave simulator. This is quite popular with the locals and visitors alike and it always packed with people. If you need to practice your surfing skills or just find the open ocean a bit scary then this is perfect for you! Other features include indoor rock climbing, rooftop go-carting and a 5D cinema.

24. Get In The Sporting Spirit

South Africans are avid supporters of our sports teams and really get into the spirit of 'backing our boys'. Durban is the home of the Sharks rugby team, a very successful South African team! We have dedicated stadiums for soccer, rugby and cricket in Durban so there is always some kind of event or match taking place.

Experiencing a South African sports match is a great way to get a feel of our nation and culture. We regularly host our national teams, the Springboks and the Proteas, as well as international teams. I always enjoy the atmosphere and love that surrounds the crowd as we wear green and gold and cheer on our teams!

25. Spot The Big 5 On Safari Featuring An African Sunset!

An absolute must do when visiting South Africa is to go on a Safari! Here in Durban and surrounding areas there are many Game Drives and Safaris you can go on so take your pick. You can easily spot our Big 5 all year around. I recommend taking an evening Safari to get a chance to witness that movie-scene-like African Sunset! It's a beautiful sight to behold.

26. Get Your Hands Dirty On The Sardine Run

A famous phenomenon that takes place on Durbans coast once a year is the Sardine Run. This is a time when 1000's of sardines migrate across our coast. 1000's of people flock to the beach to watch them swim past like a huge wave, flopping and splashing out of the water. People also use this time to do a little fishing!

27. Appreciate Some Of The Best And Funniest Sand Art Around

It is common to find areas of the beach cordoned off for sand art as you walk along our beach. These sand artists are very talented, often creating interactive art such as couches to sit in, fine dining settings or convertible sports cars. You can have your picture taken with the exhibits for a fantastic holiday memory. Sometimes the artists take to showing off their political views with funny portrayals of South African current affairs! It's always a fun stop in your day.

28. Take A Rickshaw Ride, You Won't Regret It

You may notice colourful 2 seater benches on 2 wheels being pulled by a colourful and happy looking man or woman, these are called rickshaws! This is a fun and quick activity to experience a little slice of our tribal culture. A ride can be as long or short as you want with prices differing according to the length.

29. Cruise The Indian Ocean

Durban offers a number of cruises that leave right from our harbor. The best part is that you can choose any amount of days you want! From 2 day weekend cruises to 9 day cruises, you choose your stay even if you're tight on time. A very popular cruise is the 3 day Portuguese Island cruise. This cruise takes you just off the coast of Mozambique to scarcely inhabited Islands where you can spend the day tanning or experiencing the local tribe culture. You can also choose to stay on the ship and enjoy one of the many activities available to you onboard.

30. Rent Out A House At Zimbali

A short 25 minute drive out of Durban is the Zimbali Game Reserve. This is a protected area which offers a 5 star hotel and full golf course on its grounds. Personally I prefer renting out one of the many private lodges that are located around the reserve, you can rent these out for varying amounts of time. From here you can hike down to the beach, golf or go animal spotting. There are strict rules that have to be followed within the Reserve and these rules are strictly enforced. It is common to spot deer or zebra grazing around within arms distance!

>TOURIST

"Many a trip continues long after movement in time and space have ceased."

– John Steinbeck

Nazeera Rawat

31. Hit A Hole In One!

Durban is also big on golfing. There about 4 golf courses dotted around the city with a few more within an hour's drive. If golfing is your thing Durban is definitely the place to make your mark! If you prefer mini golf we have that too, both indoor and outdoor courses.

32. Spend A Night At The Races

Night racing is an exciting event here in Durban with many people making an evening out of it. Greyville Racecourse often holds night time racing as part of their regular schedule. Whether or not you would like to bet on the race, attending a night race is an amazing and exciting experience!

33. Catch A Fish, There Are Plenty!

A very common pastime in Durban is, of course, fishing! You will routinely spot fisherman in the early hours of the morning and all through the day set up their poles at the end of the piers at the best fishing spots. Most of these fisherman are locals fishing for fun so feel free to ask them to let you have a go! Most often any fish caught are let back into the ocean and not harmed.

34. Wander The Art District

The art district in Durban is fairly small but very interesting to drive around in or walk through. There are many art galleries you can visit but there is also a magnitude of street art, graffiti and installations to tickle your fancy. The art district is also dotted with unique artisan cafes, restaurants and shops. Well worth spending an afternoon exploring!

35. Attend An Expo

One thing Durban has no shortage of are Expos! The Durban Exhibition Centre hosts many expos scattered across the whole year. Some of these include the House and Garden Show, the Food and Wine show, Top Gear and many souks and fairs including The Eastern Bridal Fair. We even host a Sexpo once a year! If you are interested in one find out when it is running and stop by. Shows usually run for 5-10 days and basic entrance tickets are usually cheap!

36. Book A Weekend At The Drakensburg Mountains

The Drakensburg Mountains make a great family weekend getaway. It is a few hours' drive out of Durban but it is worth the drive! Here you can hike, enjoy springs, mountain climbing and basically any outdoor sport or activity you can think of. The Drakensberg Mountains are a world heritage site and therefore is also a protected area. This means you can enjoy getting up close and personal with nature and the wildlife! It is common for it to snow here during winter and temperatures do drop quite low so don't forget to bundle up a bit if you're visiting during the winter months.

>TOURIST

37. Explore Durban's Historical Sites, Architecture and Museums

Durban is home to many historical sites, amazing architecture dating back to colonial times and some really cool Military and Maritime Museums. Our city center features beautiful buildings including the main post office building, City Hall and The British Museum. We also have a Holocaust Museum situated near the beach front. If you don't mind creepy vibes you can also explore abandoned prisons and hospitals!

38. Feel Like A Giant As You Walk Mini Town!

An activity that always attracts a lot of people is a small place (literally) called Mini Town! Located on the beachfront, this place allows you to walk the whole of Durban in just a few short minutes. The miniaturised city is great for people of all ages and features all major landmarks and building in Durban. It's also a great place for photo ops!

39. Tweet Surrounded By 100's Of Species Of Birds

If you are a bird enthusiast then The Umgeni Bird Park should definitely be on your list of things to do in Durban. With 100's of species of birds to admire it is sure to keep you occupied for hours. Tickets are available at the door and there is parking available on site. Beware! The toucans bite! Make sure to keep your fingers outside the wire mesh at all times because I can vouch that getting your finger bitten is not pleasant!

40. Picnic At Mitchell Park

Mitchell Park is a favourite destination for weekend outings and picnics. It is located very near to Florida Road as well where you can get food. The park is large, very shady and provides tables and benches if you prefer not to sit on the ground. There is a children's play area with swings and such. A nice feature is the presence of a small zoo on site. This zoo has quite a variety of animals and makes a fun addition to your day.

>TOURIST

"Not all those who wander are lost."

– J.R.R. Tolkien

Nazeera Rawat

41. Rock Out To Local Music Every Sunday at Botanical Gardens

This is an activity much loved by the locals and it is easy to see why! Every Sunday afternoon at the Durban Botanical Gardens there is an outdoor concert near the lake called Music at the Lake. South African artists both nationally and internationally famous as well as newcomers perform here every week. Sometimes even international artists perform! Tickets are cheap but there are a limited number available. Make sure you bring something to eat and a blanket to sit on as the vibe is usually pretty chilled out.

42. Glam Up For The Durban July Event!

The Durban July is an event many South Africans wait all year for. It is attended by people across South Africa who flock to Durban during this time. The event is known for showcasing unique and eccentric designer wear. Tickets can be expensive but includes entrance to the event and horse racing on the day. If the fancy vibe isn't your thing there are many after-parties you can attend, arguably what people are really waiting for!

43. Hop On The Durban City Open Top Bus Tour

I recently got to host a friend from Switzerland but all she had time for was just one full day here in Durban. I spent some time pondering the best way to get her to see the whole city in a limited amount of time and decided on this bus tour. It was great! We got to see the whole city in just a few hours and it was cheap! There is a little bit of commentary but it's very basic. The tour leaves from the beachfront twice a day every day.

44. Soak Up Panoramic Views From The Cube Lookout

This spot is amazing to get views of the beach and Moses Mabhida stadium. It's got a monument on the side called The Cube but the real attraction is the view. The spot isn't on any public transport routes so you may have to take a cab but it is worth it!

45. Join An AstroTurf Soccer Match

This is something that usually happens spur of the moment but it's a ton of fun! Durban is dotted with countless Astroturf courts. Boys and girls of all ages book these hourly to play mini games of soccer or mini tournaments. Such is life that often a team is one or two players short, sometimes people drop out or get injured. That's your chance! Teams will look for people to join them, often inviting whoever is walking by or hanging out at the courts. It's a great atmosphere and experience.

46. Treat Yourself To A Spa Day At Camp Orchids

Camp Orchids is an estate located about 20 minutes outside of Durban. It includes a wedding venue, some activities and a spa. The estate also stables horses. The reason I love the spa there is because its serene and peaceful and you are surrounded by beautiful grounds. It really is the perfect environment to relax and enjoy pampering yourself!

47. Zip-Line Across Oribi Gorge

If I had to recommend one adventure as a MUST do it would be zip-lining across Oribi Gorge! I will admit it is scary at first and I almost didn't do it but I'm glad I did it in the end. I would have regretted it if I didn't! there are 2 options here, you can take the single zip-line which is a shortcut and takes you along the gorge or you can do the full 14 line zip course. I recommend doing the full 14! The first half will get you right to the edge of the gorge and then you zip across! The other half gets you back down. It's an amazing experience with amazing views, though it does take some strength as you are responsible for slowing yourself down. I did it in the rain so they operate in almost all weather conditions. You can also hike up to the rope bridge and walk across the gorge to a viewing deck. Not for people afraid of heights!

48. Explore Castle On Main

I found this gem by accident one day. I was driving the outskirts of Durban and saw a castle like building nestled on the side of the road. I turned in and noticed a café and some quaint little shops. I decided to go in and grab a coffee and ended up chatting to the server who mentioned that the upstairs was unfinished and has been abandoned for quite some time. The best news being that if I wanted to explore I was welcome to! It was a little creepy to climb up but I really enjoyed the experience. As an avid photographer it was like gold to me! The café downstairs has an amazing vegetarian and vegan menu which you should check out whether you want to explore the castle or not.

49. Light Up Your Life At The Umhlanga Lighthouse

About 25 minutes out of Durban you will find our restored but unused lighthouse. It's a popular spot for locals as there are many restaurants around the area. You are able to walk right up to the lighthouse and the beach is just beyond it. It's one of the prettiest places you could visit!

50. Water Sport To Your Hearts Content

Dams, dams and more dams! Durbanites LOVE to utilize their dams to the fullest. There is not a day when the water is free of boats, jet skis, canoes and many other things! You will be hard pressed to find a water activity you cannot do at the dam.

They even have ab-sailing and zip-lines that end mid dam making you have to let go! Many activities are available for a fee, many are free and many only require you to hire the equipment. All that aside, it's easy to make friends and get invited to tag along. Many families own boats and other water equipment and are only too happy to have you along. The more the merrier!

Top Reasons to Book This Trip

- **Beaches**: Some of the best beaches in the world.
- **Food**: Amazing fusion of foods unique to South Africa.
- **Rainbow Nation**: A rich heritage of tradition and culture all under one nation.
- **Weather**: Beautiful weather all year around!
- **People**: The best and most friendly people you will ever meet!
- **Value for money**: Definitely a place you can get the most out of your trip!
- **Great for a family holiday**: There is something for everyone! Whether you want to be active, relax, explore, eat or play.

Nazeera Rawat

GREATER THAN A TOURIST

Visit GreaterThanATourist.com

http://GreaterThanATourist.com

Sign up for the Greater Than a Tourist Newsletter

http://eepurl.com/cxspyf

Follow us on Facebook:

https://www.facebook.com/GreaterThanATourist

Follow us on Pinterest:

http://pinterest.com/GreaterThanATourist

Follow us on Instagram:

http://Instagram.com/GreaterThanATourist

Nazeera Rawat

GREATER THAN A TOURIST

Please leave your honest review of this book on Amazon and Goodreads. Thank you.

We appreciate your positive and negative feedback as we try to provide tourist guidance in their next trip from a local.

>TOURIST

GREATER THAN A TOURIST

You can find Greater Than a Tourist books on Amazon.

Nazeera Rawat

>TOURIST

> TOURIST

GREATER THAN A TOURIST

WHERE WILL YOU TRAVEL TO NEXT?

Nazeera Rawat

> TOURIST

GREATER THAN A TOURIST

Our Story

Traveling is a passion of this series creator. She studied abroad in college, and for their honeymoon Lisa and her husband toured Europe. During her travels to Malta, an older man tried to give her some advice based on his own experience living on the island since he was a young boy. She thought he was just trying to sell her something. When traveling to some places she was wary to talk to locals because she was afraid that they weren't being genuine. She created this book series to give you as a tourist an inside view on the place you are exploring and the ability to learn what locals would like to tell tourist. A topic that they are very passionate about.

Nazeera Rawat

> TOURIST

> TOURIST

GREATER THAN A TOURIST

Notes

Printed in Great Britain
by Amazon